Atchor Matthew

Before Your Exit

Building Blocks For Lasting Legacies
in Leadership

Before Your Exit
By Atchor Matthew

ISBN: 978-978-938-212-5

Published and printed by:
Stay Alive Int'l
11, Olowu Street, P. O.Box 22626,lkeja
Lagos, Nigeria
+234-8098220369, 8029309859
stayaliveintl@gmail.com

Unless otherwise indicated, all scripture quotations are taken from the New King James Version of the Holy Bible.
Scripture quotations marked KIV are taken from the King James Version of the Holy Bible.
Scripture quotations marked NLT are taken from the New Living Translation.

DEDICATION

I humbly dedicate this book to my God, the Almighty, the Strength of my living.
To my lovely wife, Ann Atchor.

And our precious children, Phebe, Emmanuela, Darlington and Great.

And to my wonderful church, Impact Centre of Church of God Mission Int'l

ACKNOWLEDGMENT

I sincerely wish to appreciate the Archbishop of Church of God Mission lnt'I Inc., Most Rev (Dr.) Margaret Benson Idahosa. Mama, the Lord shall continue to strengthen you.

I thank My Bishop, RT Rev. (Dr.) & Rev. (Mrs.) S. F. Ugbah. With you at my back, the road is much smoother.

I acknowledge my mentor, father and friend, Rev. S. O. Attah. Your love and counsel is awesome. My father, Rev. J. Aseln, your leadership is leadership. Thank you Sir!

To my sweetheart, Ann Atchor, I say thank you for letting me borrow out of your time to put this book together.

Pastor Doro Kennedy in Germany, I very much appreciate you. You laid the foundation of this work and indeed nurtured it. May the Lord bless you richly.

I dearly appreciate Rev. (Dr.) S. Ifere for his contribution to this book. Pastor Foluke Ademokun, thank you for creating time to edit this work and for your kind contributions.

And Sis Grace Uwajeh, thanks for all your efforts in publishing this book.

I also appreciate all the members of Church of God Mission Int'I, Impact Centre, Ojodu, Lagos. This grace of Our Lord Jesus Christ shall continually abide with you.

And above all, I bless the Almighty God for the revelation, wisdom and grace that is ever present.

- Atchor Matthew

CONTENT

Introduction

One of the strongest and unambiguous commands of our Lord Christ was that we should bear abiding fruits knowing well that the end of a thing is better than the beginning.

As ministers and leaders called to the service of the Master, it is imperative that we take necessary decisive steps to ensure that our work, our ministries are built on solid foundations, because a time cometh that you shall pass on the baton of leadership or elect someone or others to run the race with you or after you.

Ending well in life doesn't mean dying well or dying old, but it means replicating yourself in another person for the purpose of continuity. As leaders, we must reproduce ourselves in at least another person.

This is a biblical pattern and the trend had sustained transition from one order in other to maintain the progression of spread of the Gospel until our Lord returns. Moses produced Joshua; Elijah produced Elisha and Jesus produced His disciples. Who would you produce? This is the core message of this book.

How and why do you need to harness the potentials of your subordinates? What are the forms of leadership? Am I a charismatic leader, a bureaucratic nerd, an autocratic leader, transformational leader or a people oriented leader? What leadership style best suit me? Why is it important to work on your would-be successor, followers, and associates to help them overcome their weaknesses?

Indeed, these issues and many other insights that would help us build lasting legacies and help us end well shall be discussed in "Before Your Exit"!

And I sincerely urge you to take steps before your exit to apply the wisdom and principles of a functional kingdom life enumerated here.

1

THE HEART CRY

The greatest problem in the world today is not leadership, but good leadership. According to Myles Munroe, "Leadership is being able to influence people to do what they originally would not do but later liked what they have done."

Leadership is the ability to influence others.

What is influence?'

Influence is the ability to affect somebody's actions, character or beliefs, especially by providing an example for them to follow, winning their admiration or making them afraid to disagree. To achieve this therefore, it requires patience, perseverance, tolerance and faith in the fellow. It could take a lot of process and time. But every good leader must know this: "A good leader must not only know where he's going but should be able to inspire others as well as to go with him."

Every leader has his follower(s) and in every leader, there is always follower-ship which the continuation of the work depends. Leader succession comes from the follower-ship. The successor is the one that keeps the vision of leader alive after his demise.

There are always two kinds of members in every congregation: members in general and members in particular.

Members in general are members who, though are regular to church activities, but do not have the capacity to succeed the Pastor in the work after his exit because they didn't follow well.

Followers or Members in particular are the ones that give themselves to training, reorientation, packaging and conformation to the vision, so that they would have been well prepared to take over from the leader after his exit.

Archbishop Benson ldahosa said: **"Success without a successor is failure in disguise"**.

In the book of Exodus 1:8 the bible says, *"And there arose a king that knew not Joseph."*

This was as a result of lack of successor. Joseph as a wise and rich leader in Egypt, but he did not model anyone to take over from

Joseph was a wise and rich leader in Egpyt; but he did not model anyone to take over from him before his death.

him before his death. Myles Munroe says, "A true leader is a model for his followers."

Because Joseph didn't raise a successor before his death, his legacy and impact faded away too soon that a new Pharaoh who came on board knew him not. This lack of successor also led to the discontinuance of his good work; there was no one to take over from him.

This is the anchor of this book: the continuity of vision, raising and modeling people who will keep the vision alive so that the vision is not buried with the visionary.

"As in every seed there is a forest, so in every follower there is a leader;" says Myles Munroe.

2

WHO IS GEHAZI?

"'And it happened one day that he came there, and he turned in to the upper room and down there. [12] "Then he said to Gehazi his servant, "call this Shunammite woman." When he had called hen she stood before him. [13] "And said to him, "say now to her; 'look, you have been concerned for us with all these care. What can I do for you? Do you want me to speak on your behalf to the king or to the commander of the army?"' She answered, "I dwell among my own people" (2 Kings 4:11-13)

"...And Gehazi answered, "Actually, she has no son, and her husband is old" (2 Kings 4:14)

The Bible called Gehazi the servant of Elisha, who served Elisha in the area of ministry. He was also an associate minister ministering with Elisha. He would have operated in the office of a prophet if he had understudied Elisha successfully. Prophet Elisha understood the calling on Gehazi, so he sometimes sent him to represent him on spiritual assignments.

"Then he said to Gehazi, "Get yourself ready, and take my staff your hand, and be on your way. If you meet anyone, do not greet him; and if anyone greets you, do not answer him; but lay my staff on the face of the child "
(2 kings 4:29)

This scripture speaks of one of Elisha's assignments to Gehazi. Before Elisha entrusted his staff of office - symbol of spiritual authority and ministry to Gehazi, he was convinced of his calling, and knew he was supposed to succeed him. Elisha allowed Gehazi the use of the staff of office because it was part of the training for his succession.

Joshua served Moses, and Moses handed him the mantle of leadership. Elisha served

Elijah, and Elijah h handed him the baton of leadership. Gehazi served Elisha, but he didn't get the baton of leadership.

In our day, Gehazi could be called an Assistant General Overseer, Vice President of a Ministry, or the Assistant Pastor of a local church. He was a minister with a great ministry. (This shall be revealed and discussed in subsequent pages).

Gehazi is a prophet who was positioned to receive Elisha's spirit in double fold. He was gifted with the spirit of discernment; this made it possible for him to know the problem of the Shunammita woman. (See 2 Kings 4:14b)

1   He was prompt to act (See 2 Kings 4:26 and Romans 12)
2   He was alive to spiritual assignments (See 2 Kings 4:31a)
3   Hs was a man of faith (See 2 Kings 4:31b)

After laying the staff on the child as instructed by his master, there was no response; yet Gehazi tried several times and the situation was still the same, and he went and told Elisha that, "the child has not awoken." That was a language of faith, which means, though the child has not woken up now, he shall soon wake up. His language has been changed from impossibility to possibility. A good leader is the one that sees possibilities when others do not.

Gehazi was loyal to his Leader, Pastor, Prophet, Overseer and to the Ministry. Remember, when Gehazi took gifts from Naaman, he did not leave to start his own Ministry; he did not break the Church because he was now rich enough to start his own. Instead, he returned to the master even after suspension and discipline.

> **A good leader is one that sees possibilities when others do not.**

Indeed, Gehazi was a man of God with a great calling.

3

ON MY VISION

"So Gehazi pursued Naaman. When Naaman saw him running after him he got down from the chariot to meet him, an aid "Is all well?" 22 And he said, "All is well. My master has sent me, saying, 'Indeed, just now two young men of the sons of the prophets have come to me from the mountain of Ephraim. Please give them a talent of silver and two changes of garments." 23 So Naaman said, "Please take two talents." And he urged him, and bound two talents of silver in two bags, with two changes of garments, and handed them to two of his servants, and they carried them on ahead of him " (2Kings 5:21 -23)

The great man of God called Gehazi, who would have taken over the mantle of leadership from Elisha, had materialism as a great weakness. He could give anything to acquire material wealth. He told lies because of his love for material things.

"A faithful man shall abound with blessings: but he that maketh haste to be rich shall y not be innocent" (2 kings 5:25, KJV)

We were first human before we received the call of God as Christians; so, every one of us has a weakness or weaknesses to deal with. As a leader whose eyes are fixed on the vision of the ministry, dealing with the weaknesses of followers is one of the important areas to be concerned with.

One of the most important ingredients of leadership is the ability to bring the best out of people. If your vision must be achievable or realized, then you must work on your Gehazi; strengthen him to overcome his weakness, otherwise, the weakness will overcome the vision.

As a leader, harness the inherent latent potentials of your Gehazi as soon as the weaknesses obscuring him are completely destroyed. Jesus said in John 15:2: *"Every branch in me that does not bear fruit he takes away and every branch that bears fruit he prunes that it may bear more fruit."*

What Jesus meant in this passage is that anything that would not work in the advantage of the vision in your Gehazi should be destroyed; and everything that is producing good results should be encouraged and enhanced for the continuity of the vision. The word 'prunes' in this Bible passage means to repair - take away what will impede the work, and activate what will improve the work.

> **One of the most important ingredients of leadership is the ability to bring the best out of people.**

Every Church leader must work on their Gehazi; help them to overcome weaknesses such as lust, greed, anger, slandering, murmuring, etc. If you are a Senior Pastor, work on your Assistant Pastor – bring out the best in him; help him to overcome the virus that is ready to infect the ministry, and be a true spiritual father to him.

STEPS TO HELP YOUR GEHAZI

Talk About His Weakness With Him:
If you do not talk about a problem, it remains unsolved. Call him and talk about it, find out the root causes of the problem and how long it has been there. Remember, details of such conversations must be kept secret; his confidence must be protected at all times.

The best legacy in life is to write ones name in a platter of gold. Remember, wind blows and washes names written on sand and sky, but names written in the heart of men will be a legacy written in gold and forever will stand out.

The best life is to engrave your name in many hearts. Don't forget that success without a successor is failure. Time is never enough, but to every purpose, God has given you the time - prioritize and order your life well for the best pursuits in life.

Counsel Him:

Counselling is not a mere talking or a pity-party show over the identified problems; but it is actually a time to address the issues and give him direction. Also, always remember to keep such issues confidential. Do not sermonize or victimize him based on the information he shares with you.

Pray With Him:

Don't pray for him, but pray with him. Take him to a quite place or a camp ground and spend some days praying about the problem. A leader must show empathy – make him understand you are in with him till he overcomes his weaknesses. By this, you will succeed in winn9ing his confidence and increasing his faith in the whole process. Myles Munroe said, ***"A leader is one who leads others to leadership"***.

These are steps to leadership. Jesus said, *"Come and I will make you..."* The word 'make you' tells us the steps must be predetermined to make and get the best out of the individual.

In Acts of Apostles, the bible says the disciples were first called Christians in Antioch: because their life pattern reminded the people in the city of Christ, they called them 'Christ-like'.

A Church leader's life must be patterned after Christ before his members can emulate him.

General Overseer, does your Gehazi talk like you yet, or act like you? I know many people religiously prefer the use of the words such as, 'talk or act like Christ'. Whichever one you prefer, we all know a church leader's life must be patterned after Christ before his members can emulate him. In fact, Apostle Paul says, *"...Be ye follower of me even as I am a follower of Christ"* (1 Cor. 11:1, KJV)

God is a good example of a great leader. He had a vision of delivering Israel from Egypt. He chose Moses, a man whose weakness was anger — who murdered an Egyptian. But God took him through the wilderness in the land of Midian for 80years. There Moses learnt to become meek, gentle and tolerant. At the end of the day God Himself called Moses the meekest man on earth.

If people serve under you s and they remain unchanged, then something is wrong with you as a leader. Worse still is when the person sewing you becomes worse than when he came to you.

We become like those we closely associate with. Charlie Jones said in one of his books, *"you are the same today that you are going to be in five years from now except for two things: the people you associate with and the books you read."*

Because of this book we will focus our attention on the people we associate with.

Man-of-God, induce Gehazi with your personality. This is what guarantees the continuity of your vision. I know of several ministries that packed up after the death of the founders. "A good leader is like a friend who understands my past, believe in my future and accept my present".

Don't allow your Gehazi's acts spur you to take decisions that will affect or kill your ministry. Don't curse your Gehazi - don't curse the man that will succeed you in ministry

There is a pathetic side to Elisha's Ministry which heads of ministries and Senior Pastors must take note of and become cautious. Don't allow your Gehazi's acts spur you to take decisions that will affect or kill your ministry. Don't curse your Gehazi - don't curse the man that will succeed you in ministry, because you are a fountain, and a fountain doesn't bring forth sweet and bitter water.

"Therefore the leprosy of Naaman shall cling to you and your descendants forever." And he went out from his presence leprous, as white as snow"
(2 Kings 5:2 7)

4

MOTIVATION

Everyone gets motivated to do one thing or the other at some point in life. Motivation is to spur or stir someone into doing something, or to stimulate ones interest to react in a certain way. When an employer wants more from his staff, he motivates them with incentives.

Leaders who want their vision to continue must learn to motivate their Gehazi in every positive and possible way.

Remember that Gehazi is a human being with needs like every other person; therefore, he must be encouraged, equipped, pruned and promoted. This is to ensure that he is not tempted to act wrongly.

Elisha killed his vision when he cursed his Gehazi and didn't prepare a successor to continue his vision. The ministry came to a halt; it ended with him, with no one to succeed him because a leprous person can not occupy the office of a prophet.

Elisha was almost at his retirement from ministry when Gehazi suddenly became the catalyst that propelled Elisha's ministry to a dead end.

In 2 Kings 13:14-21, the Bible reveals how Elisha became sick, died and was buried. I want to emphasize verse 21. The Bible says, ***"So it was, as they were burying a man, that suddenly they spied a band of raiders, and they put the man in the tomb of Elisha; and when the man was let down and touched the bones of Elisha, he revived and stood on his feet"***.

This isn't just a show of miracle in the grave, but a revelation of how Elisha died and was buried with his anointing - he did not transfer it to anyone.

Elijah transferred his anointing to Elisha; Jesus transferred His to His disciples, and Katherine Kumar transferred hers to Benny Hinn, etc.

Please don't die with your anointing. Don't curse your Gehazi, because it could possibly lead to the end of your vision and impact in life.

"And he said, "All is well. My master has sent me, 'Indeed, just now two young men of sons of the prophets have come to me from the mountains of Ephraim. Please give them a talent of silver and two changes of garments" (2 Kings 5 :22)

If your Gehazi has not risen to your level of spiritual maturity, please don't impose so much on him. If you do, he certainly will obey you when you there and disobey you when you are not.

Elisha as a prophet of God lived on freewill offerings, gifts, and sacrifices offered to God, over which he had the prerogative to use as deemed fit to him. The Shunammite woman gave him a well furnished house and food, which he accepted. But in the case of Naaman, he asked him to go with his gifts (he rejected it). Though the Bible did not state why, neither did it tell us Naaman's gift was a sin.

Please don't die with your anointing. Don't curse your Gchazi, because it could possibly lead to the end of your vision and impact in life.

Elisha applied discretion - a good sense of judgment in the case of Naaman for reasons best known to him. But was Gehazi spiritual and sensible enough to understand his master to this point?

Man-of-God, you have the power to resist such gifts. But can your Gehazi resist?

As leaders, we must not be self-centered. We must learn to consider those working with us in every decision we make. Let's not assume our Gehazi understands - rather, let's always carry them along with empathy.

When I was working in the office of Gehazi between 1991 and 1998, a lot of pastors were promoted while I remained in the same position still. One day, a ministry approached me and promised to give me a three bedroom flat, and also offered to pay me four thousand naira (N 4,000) every week. This means in a month I would be earning sixteen thousand naira (N16,000), with a car. This was pretty attractive and big then.

Meanwhile, my church gave me a single room I apartment which was far away from my church, and my salary at the end of the month was less than four thousand naira (N 4,000).

The difference in remuneration was awesome. It was enticing, but I did not accept the offer. Yes, I rejected it. I am sure if it were some other persons in the position of Gehazi in a ministry as I was then, he or she would have gladly accepted it. But if I had accepted that offer, it could have affected my ministry.

I know of a senior pastor in a ministry who is fond of delaying pastors' recommendation and reports that could earn them promotion in ministry. Because of his lackadaisical approach to pastors' issues, junior and associate pastors don't enjoy working with him. If you ask any young pastor to work with him, they usually feel reluctant. When people believe in your leadership, your work will prosper.

When people believe in your leadership, your work will prosper.

What about the senior pastor who is good, powerful and hard working, but he does not understand the needs of his

Gehazi? There is a pastor in the office of Gehazi, when members remit vows, pledges or tithes to him, he tampers with it and later ask for subtraction from his allowance. Man-of-God, motivate your Gehazis!

Make sure they are duly promoted and see to their welfare and that of their wives and children.

If your Gehazi is motivated, he will take the world for you and remain loyal to you. Take him out; equip him mentally by taking him along with you to conferences. Don't let him look like a servant. Give it him opportunity even in the public. Also upgrade his living standard and appearance. When these are done, the vision can be guaranteed to blossom sufficiently even in the aftermath of your exit.

> **If your Gehazi is motivated, he will take the world for you and remain loyal to you.**

"l want you to know that people judge our organization by the way our personnel look". Finally, leaders should be motivated by their love for people and not by their desire to be great.

5

ON MY DESTINY

If you were asked, "where are you going or what is your destiny?" Can you give certain or assured answer without wavering? Truly, many people may not know their destiny even if they are actually on the path of destiny, because many people simply do not know what destiny means.

What is destiny? Destiny means a point of arrival - a place where dreams become a reality.

From the Bible, we can glean that Gehazi had a desire to become what his master wanted of him. He went where he was sent, in anticipation of getting to his destiny.

"Now, Gehazi went on ahead of them, and laid the staff on the child..." (2 Kings 4:31)

This was the dream of Gehazi - to be able to use the staff that was soon going to be handed to him to do times two of what Elisha did in his life time.

Elisha was used of God to do so many mighty works. So, Gehazi was also expecting and praying to God to mightily use him in a similar way. This is the desire of every minister of God called into the ministry - to do greater works than his predecessor.

"Most assuredly, I say to you, he who believes in Me, the works that I do he will do also; and greater works than these he will do..." (John 14; 12)

"For I know the thoughts that I think toward you, says the Lord, thoughts of

God has great plans for you and His work. There is already a provision of grace for greater works. Greater works means you will do more than your predecessor. Jesus healed the sick, raised the dead by spoken words, and sometimes by forming clay with His saliva He opened a blind man's eyes. At other times, when the crowd around Him was too much, they just touched the helm of His garment and they were healed.

But in Peter's dispensation, the sick, blind, lame and dead had no need to come to him or touch his clothe. They just waited for him on the way at strategic routes which they knew he certainly would pass, and as his shadow fell on them, great miracles took place. This is greater works Jesus told us of.

Apostle Paul didn't need to be present for a miracle to break forth. All he did was to send his handkerchief or apron and the miracles happened. This is greater works.

One great man of God was said to have walked into a factory, and every worker at sight started confessing their sins, and some were slain in the spirit. This is greater works.

We have seen large crowds at Billy Graham's crusades, who from a simple message of "'Jesus loves you" were spurred with godly sorrow unto repentance during altar calls. That is greater works!

We also know of Arch Bishop B.A. Ildahosa and how he confronted the World Congress of Witches & Wizards and declared that their meeting scheduled to hold in Nigeria should not hold, and it didn't hold. Elijah dealt with 450 prophets of Baal in Israel.

> **This is the desire of every minister of God called into the ministry - to do greater works than his predecessor.**

Idahosa dealt with millions of demons and their agents all over the world. This is greater works!

In 1988, Papa E. A. Adeboye's Holy Ghost Congress which held at Lekki witnessed over three million people in attendance. That is greater works.

What about the largest single church auditorium in the world – 'Canaan Land', in Otta, Nigeria? It was built in a village that has metamorphosed into a city. Canaan Land has all it takes to be called a modern city and lack nothing. This is greater works.

The list goes on; but I want us to regress a bit to the task before us, which is the need to align ourselves with biblical requirements that qualify a man for greater works. The question today is, "'do you want to remain where you are?"

It is time to work on ourselves so that we can accomplish the task before us and fulfill our destinies. Our greatest enemy in this quest is self.

Until we deal with self, we will not get to our destiny.

Until we deal with self, we will not get to our destiny. Gehazi had a great vision for the ministry, but he couldn't really deal with his weaknesses.

> *"But Gehazi, the servant if Elisha the man of God said, "Look my master has spared Naaman, this Syrian, while not receiving from his hands what he brought; but as the Lord lives, I will run after him and take something from him" (2 Kings 5:20)*

Gehazi's weakness was greed and lust for materialism. He refused to address this area of his life. And it is very true that, what you don't conquer will consume you and destroy your destiny.

Gehazi had a great vision for the ministry, but he couldn't really deal with his internal problems.

Man-of-God, look at yourself and be very sincere with yourself. What is that weakness of yours that is capable of consuming your ministry, vision and dreams? Deal with it; go to God and ask Him to help you.

Is your ministry important to you'? If yes, then terminate these habits also known as 'The Enemies of Ministerial Success'. As you approach ministerial goals, you need to do daily self-evaluation and make adjustments from greed, lust, anger and insubordination.

This change is essentially necessary for success in ministry and life, no matter how small it is.

The psalmist declared, ***"The LORD will perfect that which concerns me..." (Psalm 138: 8).*** Yes the Lord is still in the business of perfecting people. But you must be ready and also create the right atmosphere for Him to work on you.

Everybody wants to change the world, but no one wants to be changed. As a minister of God, before you can change your world, you need to be changed.

*"**Better to be pruned to grow
than cut up to burn**"*
- John Trapp

*"**Bad habits never go away by itself; it's
always an undo-it-yourself project**"*
- Abigail Van Buren

The level of anointing has nothing to do with what we are saying here. Remember, 'wild flowers don't care where they grow'. So be wise if you want to experience ministerial success. Pay attention to yourself. Deliberately bring yourself under self evaluation and discipline because the road to success is always under construction.

As a minister of God, before you can change your world, you need to be changed.

Many great ministries and ministers are no more today because of little things they failed to do. Judas Iscariot was in the ministry of Jesus Christ just like the other twelve disciples, but he ended up as a failure because the love and greed for money derailed him.

Gehazi, the servant of Elisha went into the ministry without conquering his weakness - this earned him leprosy. Simeon's ministry died in the wilderness because he did not conquer anger. And so many ministers and leaders have failed because of pride. W.L. Mordy said, ***"Be humble or you'll stumble!"***

As a minister of God, before you can change your world, you need to be changed.

Man-of-God, your future and success in ministry depends on a lot of things; but I want you to take note of this instructive truth: ***"True character is s made in secret and displayed openly."***

6

FOLLOWING TO BECOME

Everyone in life wants to be made; but it is not everyone that is willing to prove his or her commitment and loyalty to the process that can make them.

In Matthew 4:19, Jesus said, ***"Follow me, and I will make you..."*** How many people truly follow their leaders?

Consistent follower-ship is usually the problem to every leadership and organization. These days, people aren't willing to prove their commitment and loyalty to anyone. The words of at Jesus in this verse of scripture are very exact and explicit - *"Follow me, and I will make you..."*

To be made is a process, and for this to be achieved the individual must commit himself to the process consistently. In other words, you must be humble, faithful and loyal to the process. This means the person must be broken and contrite in spirit. His ego must be broken in the process.

If you don't follow well you cannot be made. If you are not a good follower, you will never be a good leader.

Before anyone can be made, he must first deny himself of so many things, even if they seem pleasurable and comfortable. And some of these things would include pride and self-conceit. This is one of the essential keys becoming a good follower. This is why Jesus emphatically said, *"If anyone desires to follow me, let him deny himself and take up his cross, and follow me" (Matthew 16:24).*

If you don't follow well you cannot be made. If you are not a good follower, you will never be a good leader.

According to Isaac Newton, ***"The reason we see far from where we are standing is because we climb on the shoulders of those who have gone ahead of us."*** Do you climb on the shoulders of your of your leaders or measure shoulders with them"? What we become in life automatically proves the status of our follower-ship.

"If you are not a good follower, you cannot be a good leader." If you can't follow, please quit the system.

Don't try to infuse or impose your own ideas. It is an act of rebellion, and it's ungodly to do such. God will always inspire the head of a ministry and give him every new idea for the ministry's new or next level. Note that God is not the author of confusion.

How To Follow Well

- **Believe In Your Leader**

2 Chronicles 20:20b says, *"...believe his prophet, and you shall prosper"*.

Also, in John 15:16, Jesus said, ***"You did not choose me, but I chose you and appointed you that you should go and bear fruit."***

Every leader must know that he didn't call himself, but God called him. God saw your weakness before He called you; therefore, followers must also look beyond the faults of leaders. We are not perfect people; but we are being perfected everyday as we hear God's word. .

According to Archbishop Benson A. Idahosa, ***"God does not call the qualified; but He qualifies the called."***

Believe in your leader because your prosperity is hinged on him. Refuse to see his inadequacies and weaknesses. Remember,

God didn't call him because he was perfect. Rather, God also wants to perfect him as He uses His servant to perfect and work on you.

- **Be Loyal and Faithful**

As I said earlier, you must prove your commitment to your leader before you can be trusted with leadership by God and man. This calls for faithfulness, sincerity and submissiveness.

If you must climb to the top, be faithful to leadership and authority, because God rewards faithfulness.

"Well done, good and faithful servant..."
(Matthew 25: 21)

God frowns at every form of disloyalty to leaders constituted authority. Indeed every attempt to usurp the role of the leader is considered a   rebellion. Rebellion connotes disloyalty to leadership or authority. And God sees rebellion the same way He sees the sin of witchcraft.

"For rebellion is as the sin of witchcraft..." (1 Sam. 15:23)

- **Be Ready To Learn**

Romans 12:9 says, **"...Cling to what is good."** In every organization there is always the good, the bad and the ugly. Remember that the Bible urges us to hold fast to what is good. Don't spend time with slanderers and other people who wouldn't rest till they slam your leader. Instead, have a teachable spirit. Be ready to learn from your leader. Studying and highlighting the faults of your leader is only an easy route to your self destruction.

Jesus in His early ministry appointed twelve disciples that would succeed Him. These disciples had to study Him. They asked questions whenever they didn't understand Him. In a short while, except for the son of Judas, their

> **Studying and highlighting the faults of your leader is only an easy route to your self destruction.**

ways of life became patterned after that of Jesus to the extent that they walked like Him and even looked like Him. This was perhaps why Judas had to kiss betrayal to enable the Roman soldiers differentiate Him from the disciples.

The pastors of Archbishop Benson Idahosa speak like him that one can hardly distinguish the voices. The same is also seen of David Oyedepo and his assistant, Bishop David Abioye.

- **Watch Against Insurgence**
"Now the sons of the prophets who were at came out to Elisha, and said, "Do you is know that the LORD will take away your master from over you today?" And he said, yes, I know; keep silent!" (2Kings 2:3)

At every point in time, Elisha was always abreast of what would happen. These sons of the   mentioned in 2 Kings 2:3 were bible scholars. They were in every city Elijah and Elisha went. They were quick to notify Elisha that his master was to be taken away.

Sons of the prophets are also everywhere in churches today. They could be found among the members, deacons, deaconess, elders, etc. But please always guide your heart against conversations that says how the senior pastor victimizes you or deny you of certain privileges. Such talks are actually meant to fill your mind with grieve and thoughtless decisions or at best, to massage your ego.

1 want you to note that Elijah never told Elisha what was going to happen to him. He did not let Elisha know the meaning of his journey from Gilgal, Bethel, Jericho and to Jordan. From the human angle, this was a good reason for Elisha to become upset and disloyal, because the man whom he assisted intentionally concealed his exit from him.

But if Elisha had allowed the sons of the prophet to come between him and his master, that would have cost him his mantle.

Man-of-God, don't let anyone come in between you and the mantle that will soon get to you. Be careful!

- **Accept Correction**

Mr. Gehazi, if your calling is so important to you, and you want to be a great man-of-God, please accept correction, for in the multitude of counsel there is safety, says the bible.

"He who is often rebuked, and hardens his neck, will suddenly be destroyed, and that without remedy" (Proverbs 29:1)

- **Be Humble**

"...God resists the proud, but gives grace to the humble" (James 4:6)

"Humble yourself in the sight of the lord, and he shall lift you up" (James 4:1 0)

Pride catalyzes failure and downfall. When there is pride in you, it makes you an enemy of God. Nebuchadnezzar, after learning his lesson said, *"...The most high rules in the kingdom of men, and gives it to whomever he will" (Dan 4:17).*

No matter how much praise you get from people, don't let it get into your head; don't let your ego dictate your manner of speech.

Don't say,"Without me nothing can move"; "people prefer me to my superior"; "1 can preach more than my superior", etc.

7

ARE YOU A MENTOR OR A TORMENTOR?

For some years now, mentor, mentorship and mentoring have become a resounding vocabulary in the lips of Christians, especially preachers. Many teachings have been expounded to authenticate this very subject. Also in reality, many young ministers have been greatly exploited in the name of mentorship by their 'Spiritual Fathers'.

Who Is A Mentor?

A wise and trusted adviser to a person is a mentor. A mentor is a mentally matured and experienced father, counselor, confidant, friend and leader. He is someone who has an edge over you in the area you are aspiring to in life.

Note that mentorship is not the same thing as sponsorship. You don't need to have only one mentor. You can actually have mentors in all or several spheres of life that you deem necessary.

Biblical Examples of Mentors
- Moses mentored Joshua
- Eli mentored Samuel
- David mentored his mighty men
- Elijah mentored Elisha
- Jesus mentored his disciples
- Barnabas mentored Paul
- Paul mentored Timothy and Titus

A mentor is someone whose hindsight can become your foresight. In biblical times, elderly ministers mentored younger ones.

Points to note:
Many ministerial casualties are due to lack of mentors.

Everyone needs someone to mentor and train him or her:
- For proper and balanced foundation
- To avoid many mistakes
- To have credibility in ministry
- For proper understanding

Methods of Mentoring: Titus 2:1 -8

Any parent with more than one child knows that every child has his or her own attributes and qualities. Before mentorship, the mentor must know that every one that submits to him or her is like a child with features and qualities that are uniquely his or hers.

Protégé: Be ready to be loyal, submissive and learn from your mentor.

Mentor: Give them what they cannot get on their own. Be a parent to them:

As a mentor, the word parent could be broken down mean:

P - Purpose: Give them purpose for living. Help them to discover their life's purpose, and purposefully invest in them.

A - Assessment: Give them honest and candid feedback. Help them access their growth level.

R - Relationship: Your relationship is the glue that holds them to you. The higher the challenges, the closer you should be to them.

E - Encouragement: Without encouragement, they might lack the needed guts to forge ahead when they fail or are in difficulty.

N - Navigation: Help them to navigate their way out of the difficult curves in life and ministry.

T - Tools: They need tools and resources that only experienced leaders can provide.

Things That Turn Mentors Into Tormentors:
(The Saul And David Example)

- Saul looked at David's every activity with suspicion

- Saul hurled his spear at David to kill him

- Saul feared David because of God's Spirit in him.

- Saul changed David's position to prevent him from seeing David or being near him

- Saul dreaded being compared to David in any way

- Saul gave David 1,000 troops in the hope that the Philistines will kill him

- Saul gave his daughter Michal to David with the hope that she would be a snare to him.

- Saul several plots against David failed
- Saul perceived himself as David's enemy

What or who are you? A mentor, or a tormentor?

It is not too late to make a change!

8

THE PROFITABLE LEADER

Leadership comes in many complexions and categories, and operates at diverse levels. There are indeed various types of leadership styles with each having its positives as well as weaknesses.

As leaders, we need to know what best reflects our attributes and how our leadership styles affect our progress as well as the well being of the people entrusted to our care. This is relevant because many people do not appreciate or understand that the little attitudes they put up as leaders either make or mar their ability to effectively lead and grow functional followers to succeed them.

What kind of leader are you'? What leadership style can best be attributed to you?

Autocratic Leadership:
This is a type of leadership where the leader exercises absolute powers over his subjects. The subjects don't have a say in the way things are done under this kind of leadership. The leader is the final authority on every issue.

Under this kind of leadership, if it is a company, it staff frequently resigns and the leadership end up spending time and energy in search of employees rather than learning to be flexible, to solve the problem.

Bureaucratic Leadership:
This is the type of leadership that worships organizational procedures. This type of leadership is good for organizations whose business or activity involves safety and risks

issues. For instance, in some factory work, airline business, banking, oil and gas, etc, where volatile substance are frequently used, and where safety issues cannot be compromised, there is always strict observance of regulations to the barest minimum.

But is this leadership style really effective in other areas especially where human relations and attitudes are prominent? Your guess is as good as mine!

Charismatic Leadership:
This type of leadership is often associated with religious groups. The leader injects enthusiasm into his followers. One problem with this type of leadership is continuity. Charismatic qualities are usually not transferable to everyone.

Task Oriented Leadership:
This type of leadership focuses on getting things done. Its goal is simply geared towards accomplishing specific tasks. And this is where its weakness is pronounced.

The task oriented leader spares very little thought for the well being of its group members or staff. It can be insensitive to their plight. A major problem with this type of leadership is the difficulty in motivating and retaining staff in the organization. Some scholars have argued that it sees and treats men as tools merely used in achieving goals.

Transformational Leadership:
This type of leadership inspires members of the group or staff of the organization to share in the vision. Transformational leaders are highly visible and spend a lot of time communicating their goals, visions and ideals. They don't necessarily lead openly; but they delegate responsibilities.

People Oriented Leadership:
This type of leadership focuses on organizing, supporting and developing the people.

An organization with this kind of leadership keeps producing leaders who positively affect every part of the society where they are present. They leave behind lasting legacies.

Note that, being people oriented leader does not mean you are a people-pleaser. It does not mean you dance to the tunes of the people all the time when you know the right thing to do. It does not mean the leader surrenders to the whims and caprices of the people when it comes to taking decisions. It simply means he is committed to the well being of his people, members or followers.

As a leader, what leadership style would you rather adopt? 1 know you wish to leave a landmark after your exit'? In essence, the people oriented form of leadership is the ideal style of leadership and I suggest you align with this pattern.

9

PROGRAMMED TO REPRODUCE

Of all things created by God, living things have a unique place in the sense that God planted the ability of self reproduction in them. He patterned the existence of living things after the law of reproduction, which is a law that simply states that every living thing must reproduce its own kind. As a rule, this is a significant underlining characteristic of living things.

God created everything in six days, and inside of every living thing that He created, He deposited a unique seed so that each created living being can duplicate itself.

"And God blessed them, saying, Be fruitful, and multiply, and fill the waters in the seas, and let fowl multiply in the earth.
[28] And God blessed them, and God said unto them, Be fruitful, and multiply, and replenish the earth, and subdue it: and have dominion over the fish of the sea, and over the fowl of the air, and over every living thing that moveth upon the earth"
(Gen 1:22, 28, KJV)

"Bring out with you every living thing of all flesh that is with you: birds and cattle and every creeping thing that creeps on the earth, so that they may abound on the earth, and be fruitful and multiply on the earth" (Gen 8:1 7)

"Release all the animals and birds so they can breed and reproduce in great numbers "
(Gen 8: 1 7, NLT)

So from creation, man is programmed to reproduce himself. Every newborn baby you see today is a product of the seed deposited in a man (the father) which he has to release into his wife to produce that child. Every fruit you eat today is not newly created by God; but it is a product residing inside of a seed already in existence. Likewise, every profession you find today is born by a professional. A teacher produced the teachers we have today; a doctor produced the doctors, and the trend goes on and on. The seed of the herb are inside of it. When it is released it produces several herbs.

"Then God said, "Let the earth bring forth grass, the herb that yields seed, and the fruit tree that yields fruit according to its kind, whose seed is in itself on the earth"; and it was so.

[12] And the earth brought forth grass, the herb that yields seed according to its kind, and the tree that yields fruit, whose seed is in itself according to its kind. And God saw that it was good" (Gen 1: 11-12)

"Then God said, "Let the land burst forth with every sort of grass and seed-bearing plant. And let there be trees that grow seed-bearing fruit. The seeds will then produce the

kinds of plants and trees from which they came." And so it was.

12 The land was filled with seed-bearing plants and trees, and their seeds produced plants and trees of like kind. And God saw that it was good" (Gen 1: 1 1-12, NLT)

The parable of the Talent in Matthew 25: 14-30 teaches a very instructive lesson. Here, Jesus told a story of a king that traveled to a far country, but gave his servants talents before he embarked on his journey.

The first servant was given five talents; the second one got two talents, while the third received one talent. Everyone was given a talent according to his ability.

Notice that the king did not tell them what to do with the talent nor was instruction given to the 5 servants to trade with the talents. This is what happened. The servant with five talents traded with it and reproduced five extra talents. The one with two talents also traded with his and produced two more talents. But the servant who received one talent did not trade with it; rather, he dug the ground and kept it there.

When the master returned from his journey, joyfully, the servant with five talents gave report of his activities and showed his master the additional talents he had made. Likewise, the servant with two talents came and showed the additional two he had made.

As any reasonable master would do, their master commended them and rewarded them.

However, the servant with one talent who dug the ground and hid it, brought his talent and gave it as it was given to him. Note the reaction of the master;

- He was angry at the servant

- He even wished the servant had given the talent to an investment company for it to yield some profits before he returned

- He took the talent from the servant and gave it to the one with five, and said, ***"For to everyone who has, more will be given, and he will have abundance; but from him who does not have, even what he has will be taken away" (Matt 25:29)***

- He decreed that the servant be executed (Matt25: 30)

So what are the lessons here'?

The master never told them what to do with the talents given. Why was this so'? Note that, from the creation of the world, God has programmed every living thing that was created to produce its kind. Therefore, the servants didn't need any instruction in this regard. Their instincts or commonsense was there to tell them the natural thing to do, which is to produce or multiply, just as two of the servants did.

Wherever you find yourself, and whatever gift or assignment that is given to you should not end with you. Endeavour to multiply and reproduce. As a matter of fact, you are not programmed for failure or that things may die in your hands. This is the very reason why God said none of us shall be barren.

"You shall be blessed above all peoples; there shall not be a male or female barren among you or among your livestock" (Duet. 7:14)

"No one shall suffer miscarriage or be barren in your land; I will fulfill the number of your days" (Exo 23:26)

As a leader or person committed excelling in life and ministry, you should never give up longing and wishing to produce a kind of yours while you are yet alive and available. If you are a follower, position yourself to be properly mentored and fashioned like your leader. Indeed, among the things that will make the Lord Jesus Christ to feel glorified and good about us and our leadership and ministry is our ability to produce other functional

workers for His kingdom. We must hunger
after this.

*"The greatest force for making people
bigger and better than they are now is
the belief in your heart and mine that
they have infinite potential for growth.
Even when they fail us, we are
to continue to carry and express
the mental image of what
they may become..."*
Dunningham

10

END WELL

"Then Elisha died, and they buried him. And the raiding band of the Moab invaded the land in the spring of the year. [21] So it was, as they were burying a man, that suddenly they spied a band of raiders; and they put the man in the tomb of Elisha; and when the man was let down and touched the bones of Elisha, he revived and stood on his feet"
(2 Kings 13:20-21)

Life is all about the legacy we leave behind and not the glamour of living a life without purpose. In the beginning, God created man and asked him to be fruitful, multiply and replenish the earth.

> **...Every leader must reproduce his kind or replicate himself.**

Man was empowered by God to reproduce his kind or duplicate himself. What this means is that every leader must reproduce his kind or replicate himself.

Ending well in life doesn't mean dying well or dying old, but it means replicating yourself in another person for the purpose of continuity. As leaders, we must reproduce ourselves in at least another person because this has been the trend since Bible times. Moses produced Joshua; Elijah produced Elisha; Jesus produced his disciples; Paul produced Timothy, etc.

> **Ending well in life doesn't mean dying well or dying old; but it means replicating yourself in another person for the purpose of continuity.**

Elisha was the only one who didn't have someone to take over from him at death. This is because the man Gehazi, who was supposed to take over from him, inherited leprosy because of his greed.

Elisha went to the grave with all the anointing of God in him because he had no successor. Remember, ***"Success without a successor is a failure!"***

Elisha had outstanding testimonies of signs and wonders in his ministries, God used him to wrought breathtaking miracles. But what happened to his ministry afterwards? Did he end well?

Let's see some of the recorded miracles God performed through Elisha.

Elisha's Miracles:
- He healed the dead and barren land

- He commanded two bears to eat up forty-two children

- He prayed for the Shunamite woman for the fruit of the womb

- He raised the dead child back to life

- He healed Naaman.

- He gave the prophecy of surplus in Samaria at a time of scarcity

- He caused blindness to come on the enemies of God's people

But with all these achievements, Elisha had no one to succeed him. When he died, his death left the nation of Israel stranded.

"True success is more of who we are than what we accomplished"
\- Steve Farrar

David showed us an example of responsive leadership. In Psalm 23:4, he says, **"Yea, though I walk through the valley of the shadow of death, I will fear no evil; for** *thou art with me thy rod and thy staff they comfort me" (Psalm 23:4)*

From this Bible passage, we find that there are two major elements and instruments every responsible leader should know and have. These are the Rod and the Staff.

The Rod

The rod is for correction. It helps a leader to correct his follower and encourage self control.

"He who spares his rod hates his son, But he who loves him disciplines him promptly" (Proverbs 13: 24)

"The rod and rebuke give wisdom, But a child left to himself brings shame to his mother" (Proverbs 29: 15)

The rod in this case is not the physical iron rod, but it means sharp rebuke, disciplinary and corrective measures put in place to checkmate an erring follower.

The Staff

The shepherd's staff is the most important instrument to the shepherd. The staff is use to guide, direct and to comfort the sheep. It is a symbol of authority.

A leader is expected to use both the rod and the staff simultaneous and equally in the mentoring of his protégé.

Leaders who use the staff more than the rod are usually considered to be real leaders, fathers, and mentor. Perhaps this is because the rod is considered to be full of punishment, hatred and unforgiveness. On the other hand, the staff is full of love, forgiveness and patience.

The psalmist said both the rod and the staff were for his comfort. In other words, both are needed in effective leadership. Leaders and fathers of ministries, you are only a success when you have your kind reproduced by you to take over from where you stopped or would stop. This is the essential proof that you have ended well.

Remember the Bible says, *"Better is the end of a thing than the beginning thereof"*.

Elisha started powerfully but ended selfishly. It wasn't too late for him to raise a successor when Gehazi erred. He still had some time to do that but he did not. He probably did not trust anyone to succeed him any longer before his death came. This is not a good sign.

Elisha perhaps could still have exerted some influence over Gehazi if he had some belief that he could remoulded him. That someone failed does not essentially mean that is the end of him.

"To have someone believe in you, even when you fail, is the most blessed and creative force in the universe"
- Dunningham

All the successes and great miracles recorded to Elisha's name and all his impact died with him.

Please take as moment and consider the following:

- Imagine what happened to Israel after the death of Elisha without a successor.

- Imagine what will happen to your ministry without duly trained successor after your exit.

- Imagine your organization collapsing after the great labour you put into it for it to get to that level it is now, just because there is no plan for transition.

Elisha was a great man of God. But he did not end well. To end well, I recommend that our Gehazi's should be led with the staff. (See chapter 3 & 4).

To end well is not to be overtly concerned about personal achievements; but it is to have your legacy inscribed in humans. How many souls have you raised that can stand and sustain your work in your absence'? It is not how many houses, cars and jets you have, or how many countries have visited; neither it is in the volume or value of the cash in your account

When Jesus ascended to heaven, it was the trained and mentored disciples that spread the gospel all over the world. Imagine if

> **To end well is not to be overtly concerned about personal achievements; but it is to have your legacy inscribed in humans.**

Jesus had cursed Peter for suggesting something contrary to the redemption plan. What would have become of the great revival in Acts chapter (3: 12) and the many others?

Jesus used the staff and said to Peter, *"...Simon, Simon! Indeed, Satan has asked for you, that he may sift you as wheat. [32] "But I have prayed for you, that your faith should not fail; and when you have returned to Me, strengthen your brethren" (Luke 22:31-32).*

What a reposing confidence Jesus had on Peter. Other pastors would have driven him away, suspended or asked him to leave their ministry, because his view is in sharp contrast to their plan. But Jesus used the staff and moulded Peter until he became like Him, his Master.

In ending this chapter, l want to encourage us to do all we can to replicate ourselves in people for the continuation of the vision which the Lord has given us.

It is one thing to have an impact and have a thriving ministry, but it is another thing entirely to leave a legacy after your exit.

Remember, Jesus Christ, your Master, your Shepherd, said, *""You did not choose Me, but I chose you and appointed you that you should go and bear fruit, and that your fruit should remain, that whatever you ask the Father in My name He may give you"*.

This simply means, the Lord wants your fruits, your work to remain, to have a lasting legacy.

1 sincerely pray that whatever would stand in your way to hinder, delay or divert you from the purpose, place and vision of God for your life and ministry, the mighty hand of God that disgraced Pharaoh and the gods of Egypt shall scatter them.

May His grace and wisdom elevate you to the heights you have dreamt of.. And may His provision and mercy sustain you all the way, in Jesus' name.

God bless you!

For More Information,
Prayers, Mentoring & Counselling,
Contact:

Rev. Atchor Matthew
+234-8023261381
email: matchor@yahoo.com
Facebook: Atchor Matthew

Or Visit
Church of God Mission Int'I Inc.
Ojodu Provincial Headquaters
(Impact Centre)
1-9B, Morgan Street,
Ojodu, Lagos, Nigeria.